THE UNIVERSE ROCKS!

GALAXIES AND THE RUNAWAY UNIVERSE

RAMAN PRINJA

QEB Publishing

To Kamini, Vikas and Sachin

Editorial and Design: Windmill Books Ltd.
Illustrator (activities): Geraint Ford/The Art Agency

Copyright © QEB Publishing 2012

First published in the United States in 2012 by
QEB Publishing, Inc.
3 Wrigley, Suite A
Irvine, CA 92618

www.qed-publishing.co.uk

A CIP record for this book is available from the Library of Congress.

ISBN 978 1 60992 244 3

Printed in the United States

Picture credits (t=top, b=bottom, l=left, c=center, fc=front cover)
ESA: 10-11; NASA: 4-5, 4bl, 6-7, 7tr, 10bl, GRIN 30-31, Hubble Site 1t, 6l, 7r, 11tr, 12bl, 12-13,
13br, 20-21, 21br, 24bl, JPL 14-15t, 28-29, 32, NIX 32; NOAA: 16tr; Science Photolibrary:
Chris Butler 16-17, Emilio Segre Visual Archives/American Institute of Physics 20bl,
Mark Garlick 26-27, Mehau Kulyk 24-25, Detlev Van Ravensway 27bl; Shutterstock:
16-17b, 19t, Viktar Malyshchyts 2-3, Sander Van Sinttruye 8-9; Thinkstock: istockphoto 23t.
*We have made every attempt to contact the copyright holder. If anyone has any
information please contact smortimer@windmillbooks.co.uk*

Website information is correct at time of going to press. However, the publishers
cannot accept liability for any information or links found on any Internet sites,
including third-party websites.

In preparation of this book, all due care has been exercised with regard to the
activities and advice depicted. The publishers regret that they can accept no
liability for any loss or injury sustained.

Words in **bold** are explained in the glossary on page 31

What is a Light-year?

Distances in space are measured in light-years.
A light-year is the distance that light travels in one year.
- In one second light travels 186,000 miles
  (300,000 kilometers) or seven times around Earth.
- In one minute light travels 11 million miles (18 million
  kilometers) or to the Moon and back 50 times.
- In one year light travels 5,600 billion miles (9,000
  billion kilometers) or one light-year.

CONTENTS

WELCOME TO THE MILKY WAY

The Sun and all the stars you see at night belong to our home **galaxy**, which we call the Milky Way.
A galaxy is an enormous collection of billions of stars, plus gas and dust held together by **gravity**.

There are **billions** of galaxies in the **Universe**. In this book we will journey to some amazing galaxies, watch enormous crashes in space, and learn about the latest mysteries of the Universe.

Seen from the side, the Milky Way Galaxy is a thin disk with a bulge in the middle.

The Milky Way

Our Home

From above, our Milky Way Galaxy would look like a giant pinwheel, with long arms of stars and **dust** clouds. From the side it looks a bit like two fried eggs stuck back to back! The Sun is just one of 200 billion stars in our Galaxy. Astronomers think that an enormous **black hole**, with 3 million times more mass than the Sun, is at the heart of the Milky Way.

Light-years Across

The Universe is so vast that the sizes and distances between galaxies are hard to imagine. Instead of using miles to measure distance, **astronomers** use a unit called a **light-year**. One light-year is the distance light travels in a year. That is about 5,600 billion miles (9,000 billion kilometers)! The Milky Way Galaxy is so big that light would take 100,000 years to travel from one side to the other. We say that the Milky Way Galaxy is 100,000 light-years across.

The bright bulge in the middle of the Milky Way is packed with lots of stars.

Scaling it Down

We can use scale models to help understand the huge sizes of galaxies. Imagine the Sun is the size of a grain of sand. The Earth would be an even tinier speck about a third of an inch (1 cm) away from the grain. Even in this tiny model, the Milky Way Galaxy, with its 200 billion stars (or grains of sand), would still be 49,700 miles (80,000 kilometers) across. That's six times wider than the Earth's diameter!

GALAXY ALL-SORTS

Galaxies don't all have the same size or shape. There are dwarf galaxies made of millions of stars and giant galaxies loaded with trillions of them.

The sizes of galaxies can be between a few thousand light-years across to several hundred thousand light-years. In the 1920s an astronomer called Edwin Hubble studied lots of galaxies and found that they looked different. There are three main types of galaxies, called spirals, ellipticals, and irregulars.

This spiral galaxy looks like ours. The Sun would be about here.

Spirals

Our Milky Way Galaxy is a **spiral** galaxy. Most of the stars, gas, and dust clouds are gathered in arms that wind out from the center of a galaxy. The whole galaxy spins like a giant whirlpool. Spiral galaxies have lots of new stars in them. About a fifth of all galaxies in the Universe are spirals.

Ellipticals

Elliptical galaxies are shaped like footballs. These galaxies are mostly made up of old stars and have much less dust than spiral galaxies. The largest galaxies in the Universe are ellipticals with **trillions** of stars.

An irregular "messy" galaxy!

Elliptical galaxy surrounded by many other distant galaxies.

Irregulars

Irregular galaxies don't have any real shape. They look like messy collections of stars, gas, and dust. Irregular galaxies are usually the smallest and have lots of bright, newly born stars in them.

Imaginary view of a Quasar.

Powering Up

Some of the most energetic galaxies in the Universe are called **quasars**. They are also among the farthest galaxies we can see in the Universe. Quasars are so far away that the light from them can take 10 billion years to reach us!

BUILD YOUR OWN MILKY WAY

The Milky Way is a spiral of stars, gas, and dust. In this activity you can make your own model of our Galaxy.

The Milky Way can be seen in the night sky as a misty band of light, full of stars.

TRY DOING THIS...

Find out about the shape of our Galaxy and the place of our Solar System inside it.

You Will Need:

* 11.8 inch (30 cm) diameter plate
* Thick black cardstock
* Pencil
* Scissors
* PVA glue
* Cotton balls
* Silver and blue glitter
* Red dot stickers
* String

1 Place the 11.8 inch (30 cm) plate on the black cardstock and draw around the plate. You will have a large circle. Ask an adult to use the scissors to cut out the circle.

Ask an adult to help.

11.8 in (30 cm)

2 Glue some cotton balls in the center of the card. Use enough to cover a space 3.2 inches (8 cm) across. Glue more balls onto the other side of the cardstock. You should have a dome shaped bulge at the center.

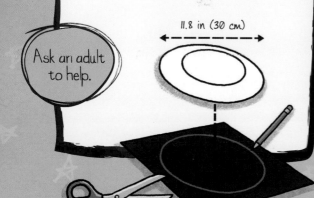

What's the Scale?

The red dot at step 5 will not be to scale. If our Solar System were scaled down to the size of a dime coin (about the size of the red dot sticker), our Milky Way Galaxy would be about the same size as Europe!

3 Pull out eight cotton balls into lengths. Glue four to each side of the cardstock. Glue them in spiral shapes that unwind from the ends of the central bulge.

4 Drip glue over all the cotton on the cardstock and sprinkle the blue and silver glitter to make some twinkling stars. Do this on both sides.

5 Take a red dot sticker and place it about 3.2 inches (8 cm) from the center on one of the spirals. The red dot marks the position of our Sun in the Milky Way.

6 Once you have finished, make a hole near the edge of the cardstock and tie string through it so you can hang your model galaxy from the ceiling. Try making some more galaxies of different sizes.

...WHAT DID YOU LEARN?

In this model, the cotton balls in the center represent the bulge of our Galaxy. More than half the stars are located here. The cotton lengths are the spiral arms of bright young stars. The red dot shows the location of our Sun and Solar System, 27,000 light-years from the center of the Galaxy.

MAPPING THE UNIVERSE

There may be 200 billion galaxies in the Universe. Scientists are using powerful telescopes to make a map showing how they are all positioned in space.

Galaxies are mostly found in groups, where dozens are held together by gravity. Imagine that you are a planet, and your house is a solar system—the other people in your family are other **planets**. Then you can think of your home city or town as a galaxy of houses. On a map of your country, the cities are different galaxies and the countryside between them is like the empty space between galaxies.

Gravity holds galaxies together, even across thousands of light-years of empty space.

Andromeda

Meet the Neighbors

The Milky Way is part of a group of 25 galaxies that includes another magnificent spiral galaxy called Andromeda. This group of galaxies is spaced out over a vast distance of about 5 million light-years. There are many other similar groups of galaxies in space.

Spongy Universe

Galaxies are not evenly spread across the Universe. The galaxies form chains that run between large bubbles of space that are almost empty. The pattern made by galaxies is a bit like the holes in a bath sponge!

Biggest Things in the Universe

Astronomers have mapped out where the galaxies are in the Universe and discovered some amazing structures. They have found that some groups of galaxies can be linked to make enormous stretched-out chains across space. Known as **superclusters**, these groups of galaxies can stretch over distances of more than 100 million light-years. Superclusters of galaxies are the largest things in the Universe. They can contain 2,000 large galaxies and 50,000 smaller ones. That all adds up to 200 trillion stars in a supercluster!

COSMIC CRASHES

Sometimes the force of gravity can bring pairs of galaxies so close that they crash together!

Large galaxies gobble up smaller ones and grow even bigger. Galaxy crashes can take hundreds of millions of years to happen, so we can't watch a full collision from start to finish. Instead astronomers use powerful telescopes to take photographs of galaxies in the process of coming together in space.

Galaxy smash

Antennae Galaxies

The Hubble Space Telescope has taken fantastic images of two galaxies that started to crash into each other a few hundred million years ago. Called the Antennae galaxies, these spiral galaxies are 75 million light-years away from us. As the galaxies crash in a head-on collision, their clouds of gas and dust get crushed together and many new stars are made.

These colliding galaxies are called the Mice because they both have long tails.

Heading for a Crash!

The Milky Way and the Andromeda Galaxy are on a collision course in space. But don't worry—it won't start happening for another 3 billion years! Today the two galaxies are more than 2 million light-years apart. But they are heading toward each other at a speed of 310,000 miles (500,000 kilometers) per hour.

There is a lot of empty space in galaxies, and the stars are far apart. Scientists think that millions of years after the crash starts, the two galaxies will eventually join into one enormous galaxy.

The bright blue rim around the Cartwheel Galaxy is a ring of new stars.

Fiery Cartwheel

Another head-on collision, 500 million light-years away, has made the Cartwheel Galaxy. A smaller galaxy plunged into the middle of a larger one. Just like ripples when a rock is thrown into a pond, the crash made a wave of gas move out from the center of the larger galaxy. The waves swept up more and more gas and squeezed it to make new stars. Two billion newly born stars are seen in a giant ring, or cartwheel, around the galaxy.

GALAXIES IN A CUP

We have learned that there are three main types of galaxy called spirals, ellipticals, and irregulars. Here we explore spiral galaxies.

TRY DOING THIS...

In this activity explore the shape of spiral galaxies and see how the arms can be made as the galaxy spins.

In a Spin

Our entire Galaxy is spinning and it takes the Sun almost 225 million years to complete one trip around our Galaxy. The Sun moves at an incredible 492,000 miles (792,000 km) every hour!

You Will Need:

* Plastic cups
* Water
* Blue food coloring
* Plastic teaspoons
* Powdered milk

1 Fill three plastic cups half full of water and add a few drops of blue coloring. Carefully lift and turn one cup in circles to make the water swirl around. Put the cup on a table while the water inside is still moving.

2 Sprinkle about half a teaspoon of powdered milk into the center of the cup. Look at the spiral-shaped patterns made by the milk powder as it swirls around.

Half full

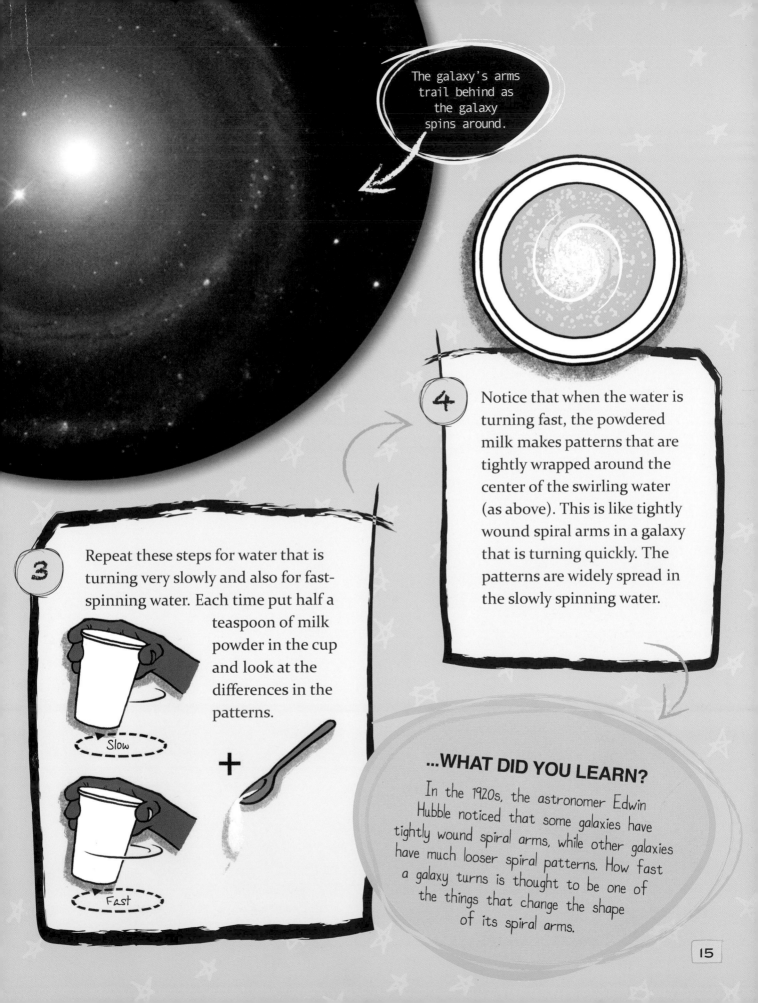

The galaxy's arms trail behind as the galaxy spins around.

4 Notice that when the water is turning fast, the powdered milk makes patterns that are tightly wrapped around the center of the swirling water (as above). This is like tightly wound spiral arms in a galaxy that is turning quickly. The patterns are widely spread in the slowly spinning water.

3 Repeat these steps for water that is turning very slowly and also for fast-spinning water. Each time put half a teaspoon of milk powder in the cup and look at the differences in the patterns.

Slow

+

Fast

...WHAT DID YOU LEARN?

In the 1920s, the astronomer Edwin Hubble noticed that some galaxies have tightly wound spiral arms, while other galaxies have much looser spiral patterns. How fast a galaxy turns is thought to be one of the things that change the shape of its spiral arms.

How Did It Begin?

Most astronomers believe that the Universe began about 14 billion years ago with a sudden explosion called the **Big Bang.**

If this happened, in less than one second the incredibly hot Universe grew from being hundreds of times smaller than a pinhead to bigger than a galaxy. The Universe has kept growing ever since, like a balloon being filled with air. After the Big Bang, as the Universe cooled down, **atoms**, galaxies, stars, and planets started to form.

A tiny fraction of a second after the Big Bang, the whole Universe would have fitted inside a grapefruit.

Cosmic Year

To understand how the Universe has changed since the beginning, let's imagine its 14 billion year history speeded up so it lasts just one year. Each calendar month equals just over a billion years.

January 1:
The Big Bang

March 31:
The Milky Way Galaxy appears

January	February	March	April	May	June

Radio waves

Big Bang

An Ancient Glow

The Universe cooled down a lot as it grew larger and larger. About 300,000 years after it began, the Universe was still five times hotter than the Sun. A glow of light was released that is still around today and fills the Universe. This glow is made up of radio waves. The radio waves were detected in the 1950s by two scientists called Arno Penzias and Robert Wilson.

December 18:
Plants start growing on land

December 24:
Dinosaurs start stomping around

December 29: Dinosaurs are extinct

December 31:
All of human history from ancient Egypt to today fits into the last 10 seconds of our cosmic year!

August 31:
The Sun and planets form

| July | August | September | October | November | December |

TIMELINE OF THE UNIVERSE

The Universe has changed over billions of years. Along the way many important events occurred, such as the birth of galaxies, the formation of Earth and the start of life.

TRY DOING THIS...
In this activity you can make a timeline to show how far apart the events in the Universe happened.

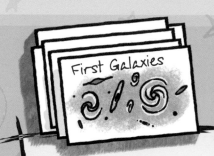

You Will Need:

* 7 index cards 4 x 6 in (10 x 15 cm)
* Long wall outside about 115 feet (35 m) or a clear floor
* One long roll of paper
* Pack of sticky tack
* Colored pencils
* Measuring tape

1 On each of the index cards write down one of these seven important events: "The Big Bang," "First galaxies," "Our Sun and the planets," "Life starting on Earth," "First dinosaurs," "First humans," "History of humans from ancient Egypt to today." Also make a drawing on each card.

Slow But Sure

Changes in space mostly happen very slowly. We have been studying the Universe with powerful telescopes for about a century, but changes in space can take millions or billions of years.

2 With help, unroll the paper roll and tack it along a wall, or floor. You will need about 115 feet (35 m) of space for this.

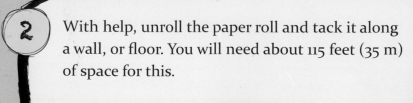

115 feet (35 meters)

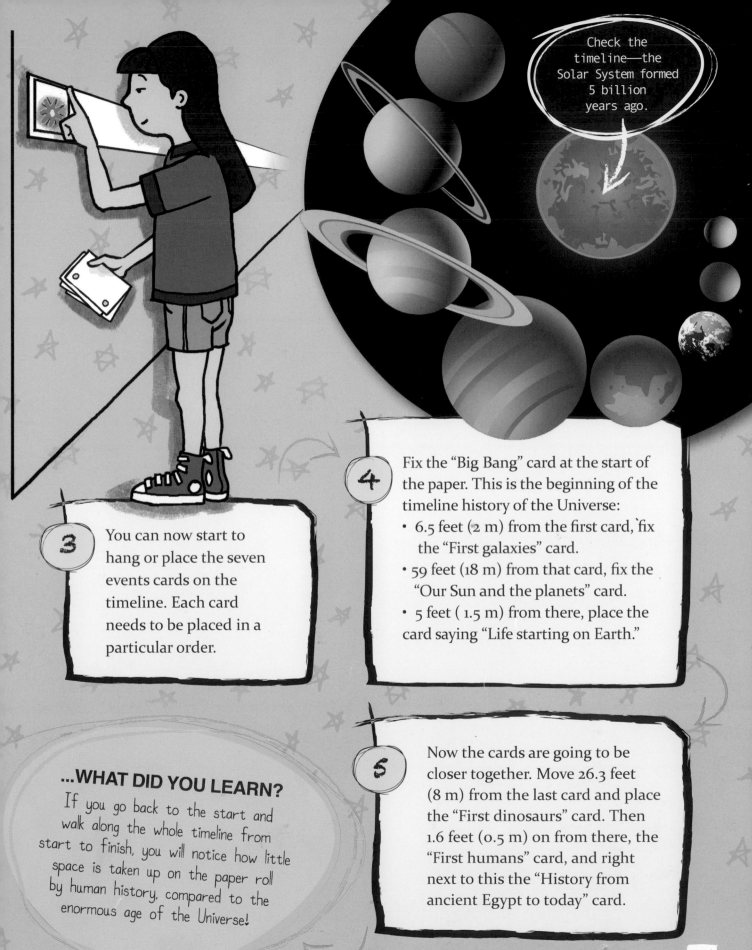

Check the timeline—the Solar System formed 5 billion years ago.

3 You can now start to hang or place the seven events cards on the timeline. Each card needs to be placed in a particular order.

4 Fix the "Big Bang" card at the start of the paper. This is the beginning of the timeline history of the Universe:
- 6.5 feet (2 m) from the first card, fix the "First galaxies" card.
- 59 feet (18 m) from that card, fix the "Our Sun and the planets" card.
- 5 feet (1.5 m) from there, place the card saying "Life starting on Earth."

...WHAT DID YOU LEARN?
If you go back to the start and walk along the whole timeline from start to finish, you will notice how little space is taken up on the paper roll by human history, compared to the enormous age of the Universe!

5 Now the cards are going to be closer together. Move 26.3 feet (8 m) from the last card and place the "First dinosaurs" card. Then 1.6 feet (0.5 m) on from there, the "First humans" card, and right next to this the "History from ancient Egypt to today" card.

Everything is Flying Apart

The Universe has been growing ever since it began. The space we see and explore is billions of times bigger than it was when the Universe was very young.

The further away a galaxy is, the faster it appears to be moving away from us. Imagine the galaxies are raisins in a cake in the oven. As the mixture heats up, it expands and each raisin, or galaxy, moves away from the others.

Edwin Hubble made his discoveries using one of the largest telescopes in the world.

Going for a Ride

In the mid-1920s when the astronomer Edwin Hubble looked at the light from galaxies, he noticed something remarkable. Nearly all the galaxies are moving farther away from each other. It's as though the galaxies are going along for a ride as the Universe grows larger. The space between galaxies is getting bigger. Edwin Hubble also discovered that the farthest galaxies are moving away from Earth faster than galaxies that are closer to us.

Age of the Universe

By looking at galaxies flying apart, astronomers know how quickly the Universe is expanding. They can also figure out how long the Universe has been getting bigger. Like playing a film backwards, we can then work out when everything was much closer together, and even when the Universe was born. Scientists think the Universe is about 14 billion years old.

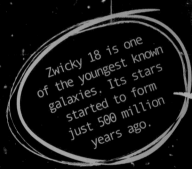

Zwicky 18 is one of the youngest known galaxies. Its stars started to form just 500 million years ago.

The color of a galaxy tells astronomers about the kinds of stars present, and their ages.

Runaway Universe

As the Universe cooled, tiny atoms formed. Gravity pulled the atoms together to make huge clouds of gas. The gas clumped together to make stars, which gathered into galaxies. Scientists expected that the gravity of all the galaxies would pull on the Universe and make it grow more slowly. But in fact the Universe is getting bigger faster and faster. No one is sure why the Universe is growing so quickly.

BALLOON UNIVERSE

Scientists think that ever since the Big Bang about 14 billion years ago, the Universe has continued to swell and expand in all directions.

You Will Need:
* A large balloon
* A permanent marker pen

TRY DOING THIS...
Make a simple model to understand how the Universe expands and why galaxies move away from each other.

1 4 in — Blow up the balloon just a little until it is about 4 inches (10 cm) across. Twist the end so that the air does not come out, but don't tie the end.

Changing Views
In ancient times people had very different ideas about the Universe. Almost 2,000 years ago the ancient Greeks thought the Earth was at the center, with all the stars and planets moving around it.

2 Using the marker, mark 10 dots on the balloon in different places. The dots represent galaxies and the balloon is the Universe. Mark one of the dots "MW," for our Milky Way Galaxy.

3 Take note of the distance between the dots on the balloon. You can think of the small balloon being the Universe when it was very young.

Astronomers believe the Universe and everything in it started with a Big Bang.

MW

8 in

4 Blow up the balloon a lot more to make it about 8 inches (20 cm) across. Look again at the spacing between the dots. You can think of the larger balloon as the Universe today.

...WHAT DID YOU LEARN?

The dots on the balloon are the galaxies going for a ride with the expanding Universe. Notice how all the dots move away from each other as the balloon gets larger and larger. This is just the way galaxies are moving further and further apart from each other. The bigger the Universe (balloon) grows, the more widely spaced are the galaxies (dots).

5

MW

Now blow up the balloon and make it bigger. You are expanding your model Universe! Twist the end of the balloon again and look at what has happened to the spaces between the dots—or galaxies.

THE DARK SIDE OF THE UNIVERSE

Scientists have found that most of the Universe is so dark and mysterious that we cannot see it even when using powerful telescopes!

More than 90 percent of the Universe is invisible. The vast numbers of galaxies are just a tiny part of it.

In this picture of a cluster of galaxies, suspected dark matter is shown in blue and the galaxies are red.

Dead Stars

Almost a quarter of the **matter** in the Universe is hidden from our view because it is too small or too cold to shine. Astronomers call this dark matter because we can't see light from it. Dark matter can be stars that have burned out and died, so they don't shine any more. There may also be lots of cold clouds of gas and dust in space that we just can't see.

Balls of gas that are too small to light up as stars are called brown dwarfs, and they can be part of the dark matter in space.

Brown dwarf

Really Strange Energy!

Almost three-quarters of the Universe is in the form of a very strange and mysterious energy called dark energy. No one is sure what this energy is or how it works. Dark energy is one of the amazing new discoveries of space. Astronomers think that dark energy is making the Universe grow faster and faster. We hope one day to understand what dark energy is and how it is pushing the Universe apart.

Strange Particles

Scientists think that the Universe is flooded with lots of strange particles that are much smaller even than an atom. Each of these particles has just a tiny mass—almost nothing—but there are so many of them that they could add up to make a large amount of dark matter.

FATE OF THE UNIVERSE

Ever since scientists have thought that the Universe started with a Big Bang, they have wondered how the Universe would end.

If the Universe has lots more matter than we know about, then it might stop growing in the future. The Universe could then start shrinking. Instead of expanding, the Universe could get smaller and smaller. It may close in on itself in a **Big Crunch**. Perhaps a new Big Bang would then start up a new Universe!

Galaxies

Other universes may be bubbles with no way to move between them.

Other Universes?

An amazing possibility is that ours is not the only universe. There could be many other universes, each with billions of galaxies and trillions of stars. But we don't know anything about the other universes because we can't look into them.

Big Freeze or Big Rip?

Instead of closing in a crunch, the Universe may instead continue to grow and stretch forever. The farthest galaxies will move even farther away from us. The Universe would get colder as it grew larger and end up in a **Big Freeze** with no heat left at all! Some scientists think that if the Universe is stretched too much by dark energy, even galaxies could start to break apart. Finally planets and even atoms would not be able to stand the stretch of space. This is called the **Big Rip**. But don't worry. If the Big Rip happens it won't start for another 20 billion years from now!

This artist's impression of the Big Crunch shows the Universe shrinking and destroying all stars and galaxies in existence.

Really Cool Stuff About Galaxies and the Universe

Galaxies and the Big Bang are important subjects. They lead to some amazing discoveries in space!

What's the Biggest Galaxy Smash?

About 5 billion light-years away a **cosmic** pileup has four galaxies colliding. Three of the galaxies are about the size of the Milky Way, while the fourth is three times as big! Stars are being thrown into space by this huge crash.

Could a Black Hole Gobble up the Solar System?

Astronomers have found a massive black hole that weighs as much as 18 billion Suns. This monster lurks in the center of a quasar. It is so big that it could swallow our Solar System whole!

Are there Great Walls in the Universe?

There are chains of galaxies hundreds of millions of light-years long. The largest known structure in the Universe is an enormous wall of galaxies that spreads across 200 million light-years. In total this gigantic wall has 300 times more matter than our entire Milky Way Galaxy.

What's Pulling the Milky Way Galaxy?

The Milky Way, along with other galaxies, is being pulled by the gravity of a mysterious object called the Great Attractor. This is so enormous that the Milky Way is flying toward it at an amazing speed of 14 million miles (22 million km) per hour!

Can you Hear Bangs in Space?

In films, explosions in space, such as stars blowing up, are given loud sound effects. The moviemakers are making up the sound! The sounds we hear every day are actually waves in the air. When the moving air reaches our eardrums, we can hear the sound. There is no air in space. Without any air, there is no sound in space either.

Are We Being Blasted with Rays from Space?

Billions of tiny particles called cosmic rays are slamming into the Earth every second. Luckily for us, the Earth's atmosphere protects us from most of them.

Are there Super-Sized Galaxies?

The largest galaxies are egg-shaped and are found in the center of galaxy clusters. This central galaxy grows by gobbling up smaller galaxies. There is a giant galaxy 5.5 million light-years across in the center of a galaxy cluster. This makes it 60 times larger than our own.

Where is the Center of the Universe?

There is no center to the Universe! The whole Universe is expanding in all directions and pushing itself away from everything else.

Did the Universe Start Really Hot?

Just one second after the Big Bang, the temperature of the Universe was 18 billion degrees Fahrenheit (10 billion degrees Celsius). It has slowly cooled over the past 13 to 14 billion years and is now a freezing -454 degrees Fahrenheit (–270 degrees Celsius)!

How Big is the Universe?

Nobody knows the exact size of the Universe because we can't see its edge. Today we can see to a distance of nearly 13 billion light-years in all directions, so it is at least this size.

TOP TEN GALAXY FACTS

1. The most distant known galaxy, UDFj-39546284, is more than 13 billion light-years away from Earth.

2. IC1101 is the largest known galaxy, with a diameter of 5.5 million light-years.

3. At a distance of 17,000 light-years, Omega Centauri is the nearest galaxy to our Milky Way Galaxy.

4. The most energetic galaxy is Markarian 231, which has a super-massive black hole at its center.

5. ISOHDFS 27 is the most massive spiral galaxy known, with a mass that is more than 1,000 billion times that of the Sun.

6. The brightest galaxy visible in the night sky is the Large Magellanic Cloud, about 150,000 light-years from Earth.

7. The spiral galaxy NGC 253 is the dustiest galaxy known, with a total amount of dust nearly 80 million times the mass of the Sun.

8. The quasar galaxy LBQS 1429-008 is really a triplet with three super-massive black holes squeezing together.

9. VIRGOHI21 is a galaxy where no stars shine. It is made entirely of invisible dark matter.

10. A record-breaking seven supernova stars have been seen exploding at the same time in the galaxy Arp 220.

WEBSITES

Hubble Space Telescope Gallery http://hubblesite.org/gallery

European Space Agency http://www.esa.int

BBC Space http://www.bbc.co.uk/science/space/

NASA http://www.nasa.gov/audience/forkids/kidsclub/flash/index.html

National Geographic Space http://science.nationalgeographic.com/science/space/

Online Star Map http://www.open2.net/science/finalfrontier/planisphere/planisphere_embedded.html

GLOSSARY

astronomer A scientist who studies objects in space, such as planets, stars, and galaxies.

atoms Tiny building blocks that make up all matter.

Big Bang A theory that says the Universe began with an enormously powerful explosion.

Big Crunch The idea that the Universe will start to get smaller and smaller and eventually collapse.

Big Freeze The idea that in the future the Universe may get colder as it grows larger and end up with no heat at all.

Big Rip A possible ending of the Universe in which all matter, including planets, stars, and galaxies, are pulled apart.

billion A very large number written as 1 followed by 9 zeros.

black hole A region of space around a very small and very heavy object inside which the gravity is so strong that nothing, not even light, can escape from it.

brown dwarf A space object that has hardly any mass and doesn't make light that we can see.

cosmic To do with the Cosmos, another word for Universe.

dust (in space) Tiny grains of solid particles found between stars.

galaxy Collection of stars, gas, and dust held together by gravity.

gravity A force that attracts two objects and which depends on the amount of matter in the objects and their distance apart.

light-year The distance light can travel in one year, which is 5,600 billion miles (9,000 billion kilometers).

matter Anything that has mass and makes up an object.

planet A large object, such as Earth, that orbits a star.

quasar A very powerful and distant galaxy that puts out lots of light.

spiral A pinwheel shape.

supercluster Made of groups of galaxies that are linked together and stretch for hundreds of millions of light-years.

trillion A huge number written as 1 followed by 12 zeros.

Universe The huge space which contains all of time, matter, and energy.

INDEX